To the reader:

Welcome to the DK ELT Graded Readers! These readers are different. They explore aspects of the world around us: its history, geography, science … and a lot of other things. And they show the different ways in which people live now, and lived in the past.

These DK ELT Graded Readers give you material for reading for information, and reading for pleasure. You are using your English to do something real. The illustrations will help you understand the text, and also help bring the Reader to life. There is a glossary to help you understand the special words for this topic. Listen to the cassette or CD as well, and you can really enter the world of the Olympic Games, the *Titanic*, or the Trojan War … and a lot more. Choose the topics that interest you, improve your English, and learn something … all at the same time.
Enjoy the series!

To the teacher:

This series provides varied readin͏g ͏ͫ ͏levels of language difficulty, from element͏

BEGINNER
ELEMENTARY A
ELEMENTARY B
INTERMEDIATE
UPPER INTERMEDIATE

GW00503018

The language syllabus has been designed to suit the factual nature of the series, and includes a wider vocabulary range than is usual with ELT readers: language linked with the specific theme of each book is included and glossed. The language scheme, and ideas for exploiting the material (including the recorded material) both in and out of class are contained in the Teacher's Resource Book. We hope you and your students enjoy using this series.

A DORLING KINDERSLEY BOOK

DK www.dk.com

Originally published as Eyewitness Reader
Time Traveller in 1999 and adapted as an
ELT Graded Reader for
Dorling Kindersley by

studio cactus

13 SOUTHGATE STREET WINCHESTER HAMPSHIRE SO23 9DZ

Published in Great Britain by
Dorling Kindersley Limited
80, The Strand, London WC2R 0RL

2 4 6 8 10 9 7 5 3

Copyright © 2000
Dorling Kindersley Limited, London

ISBN 0-7513-3178-3

Colour reproduction by Colourscan, Singapore
Printed and bound in China by L. Rex Printing Co., Ltd
Text film output by Ocean Colour, UK

The publisher would like to thank the following
for their kind permission to reproduce their photographs:
Key: b=bottom, t=top, r=right

AKG (London) Ltd: 27t, 27b, 39; Bridgeman Art Library: 20;
C.M. Dixon: 7b; Dorling Kindersley Picture Library/British Museum:
19t; /London Planetarium, Madame Tussauds: 42; /Musée du Louvre:
23br; /National Maritime Museum: 16–17b; NASA/Kennedy Space
Center: 45t; Peter Newark's Pictures: 32b, 35b, 41; Science
Photo Library: 45b, 46; Topham Picturepoint: 37b.

Additional credits: Luciano Corbella, Eugene Fleury, Gerald Wood,
John Woodcock (additional illustrations); Ermine Street Guard
(artefacts p8); Peter Anderson, Paul Bricknell, Peter Chadwick,
Stephen Conlin, Andy Crawford, Geoff Dann, Michael Dunning,
Christi Graham, Alan Hills, Colin Keates, Dave King, Liz McAulay,
Nick Nicholls, Philippe Sebert, Karl Shone, James Stevenson, Matthew
Ward, Jerry Young (photography for DK); Liz Moore (picture research).

Jacket credit: NASA: main image br

Contents

DK ELT Graded Readers

INTERMEDIATE

TRAVELLING THROUGH TIME

Written by
Caroline Laidlaw

Series Editor Susan Holden

London • New York • Delhi • Sydney

History Lesson

On a fine July afternoon, in a typical London secondary school, a class of students had just finished a history lesson. All of the students had left the classroom except for a boy and a girl, who were talking with their teacher, Mr Johnson. "Sophie," he began, "how long did you spend on your homework last week?"

"About an hour," the girl replied. "Did I get a good mark?"

"No, you didn't. I asked you to write about the most exciting event of the last 2,000 years. But you wrote about the 1966 World Cup!" said Mr Johnson. "Couldn't you think of anything more exciting? You weren't even born in 1966!"

"Well, I didn't have any ideas, so I asked my dad. He watched it on television when he was my age, and he said it was the most exciting thing that he'd ever seen."

"Sir, I couldn't think of anything to write either," Jake admitted. "I'm afraid I didn't do the homework. History's just too boring!"

"I agree," said Sophie. "History is only about dates and facts. It's really boring!"

"But I agree with you as well," said Mr Johnson. "If history was only about dates and facts it would be very boring. But it's about all sorts of people, including teenagers just like you. What is a 'fact' anyway, Sophie?"

"A 'fact' is that England won 4–2 in 1966. My father told me so. That's a real fact."

"But if your father was German, instead of British," said Mr Johnson, "he would remember that Germany lost 4–2. He wouldn't think that match was the most exciting event he'd ever seen. If your father was Hungarian, perhaps he'd say the most exciting football 'fact' was the time Hungary beat the 'unbeatable' English team 6–3 in 1953."

"And if Sophie's dad was Brazilian," interrupted Jake, "he'd tell her that Brazil won the World Cup four times, not just once like England!"

"Well, history wouldn't be boring if it was just about sport," said Sophie.

"Yes, but sport began before the 1966 World Cup, you know," said the history teacher. "Sport has played a part in much bigger historical events."

"Really, Sir? Can you tell us about it?" asked Jake, looking interested.

"Not now," replied Mr Johnson. "It's late. Come back tomorrow, and I'll show you a CD-ROM about history. You might find it rather interesting."

Ancient Rome

The next day, Sophie and Jake went to see Mr Johnson. "I've got the CD-ROM I told you about," he said. "It's from a computer company. They want to know if my students like it. First, do you remember what we were talking about yesterday, Sophie?"

"Sport before 1966! We were talking about sport and the exciting events of the last 2,000 years."

"That's right. Now, here's a question for you: if you were alive in Europe 2,000 years ago, which city would be the most exciting place to live in?"

"London, of course," answered Jake without hesitation.

"Really? 2,000 years ago London was just a collection of huts beside a muddy river. I think Rome was much more interesting. People used to say 'all roads lead to Rome' because it was the capital city of a vast empire. It contained most of Europe, North Africa and a lot of the Middle East. Eventually, it even contained Britain."

"What about sport?" asked Jake. He was getting impatient. "What sport did they have in Rome?"

"Just a minute – we're coming to that," said Mr Johnson.

He switched on the computer, put in the CD-ROM, and started the program. There was a click and a whirring noise. The screen lit up while some coloured letters spelled out "WHIRLIGIG". Then a creature with bug eyes appeared. "I'm Whirligig," said a squeaky voice. "I can move backwards and forwards through time. Just type in your favourite subject."

"S, P, O, R, T," Jake typed in quickly. The letters O, P, R, S, T, appeared on the screen in an alphabet. They were brightly coloured. Then they danced up and down, and there was some music. The letters changed their order and made the word "SPORT".

Whirligig began to spin. Rings of numbers ran around the screen.

"They're dates!" said Jake.

"AD 110," read Sophie as the rings opened out, showing a great city. "Wow!"

"Ancient Rome," said Whirligig. "For 500 years it was the capital of one of the greatest empires the world has ever

Whirligig

known. It was ruled by powerful emperors. One of them built the Colosseum – a huge amphitheatre with seats for about 50,000 people. Here, the Romans watched cruel and bloodthirsty entertainments. They put fierce, hungry lions in the arena with slaves or Christians, and they cheered as the human victims were savagely killed.

The Circus Maximus was even bigger than the Colosseum. It was the best place for chariot races, although one Roman poet said it was also the best place to find yourself a girlfriend.

Model of ancient Rome

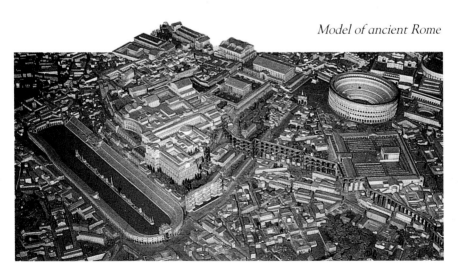

Circus Maximus, the racetrack, is on the left of the picture.

The Romans had enormous armies," said Whirligig, "with soldiers who were strictly disciplined and highly trained. The army had many legions of marching soldiers, called infantrymen. They wore armour and carried weapons and heavy packs. They could march for 30 kilometres in a day. At night, when they camped, they built ramparts around the camp for protection. Soldiers had a tough life, but they could earn quite a lot of money.

The Romans constructed long straight roads for their soldiers to march on. With strong armies and good roads, it wasn't difficult for them to conquer so many lands. Everywhere they went, they built new cities and developed trade and industry ..."

"This isn't about sport," interrupted Sophie. Then she typed the word again: "S P O R T".

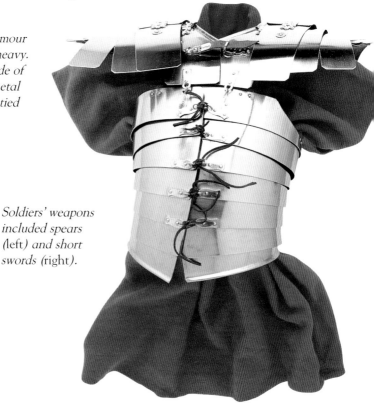

Roman armour was very heavy. It was made of strips of metal that were tied together.

Soldiers' weapons included spears (left) and short swords (right).

Roman Empire

The city of Rome was built in 753 BC. Later, by 275 BC it ruled Italy and began to expand. By AD 117, Rome was at its most powerful. It ruled all the lands shaded on this map.

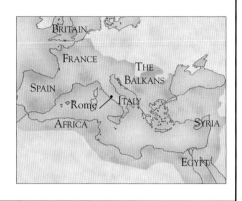

"All over the empire," Whirligig continued, "people went to amphitheatres to watch sports in their spare time.

Chariot racing was extremely popular. It was as exciting and glamorous as today's Formula One car racing. But instead of Ferrari and McLaren, the teams were called the Whites, Reds, Blues, and Greens. The unfortunate drivers – the charioteers – weren't highly paid stars like Michael Schumacher. Most of them were slaves. If they won a lot of races they could buy their freedom.

But chariot racing was a very dangerous sport. Charioteers often fell off their chariots and were stamped on by horses. Even worse, sometimes the other charioteers hit them with whips because they wanted to make them crash.

The real stars were the horses – the Emperor Caligula had one called 'Speedy' who lived in his own house with his own slaves to serve him!

Rome was an exciting city, and the sport there was really exciting. But it was also dangerous and, sometimes, not very honest. People paid a lot of money: they wanted their favourite charioteer to win."

"If you'd like to watch a Roman chariot race," said Whirligig, "click the video button on the screen."

"Here we go then," said Sophie as she clicked the button. The screen showed a close-up of a racetrack.

Around an arena there were rows of seats rising to the sky. People were moving towards their places. Two boys were walking side by side, talking about the main chariot race, which they had come to watch. They were holding blue flags belonging to their favourite teams. "Marcus only needs to win one more race," said one of the boys, "then he'll have enough money to buy his freedom."

A man with a white flag was standing behind the boys. He was listening to their conversation.

"Slaves shouldn't get their freedom," he interrupted rudely. "Who would do all the work if there were no slaves?"

The boys didn't answer. As they walked away they heard him shout, "Watch Gaius – he'll win! He's the best charioteer, and he's in the White team. Even the Emperor supports the Whites!"

Sophie laughed. "It's just like a football match today," she said. "And look at the crowd. They're eating oranges instead of hamburgers! I'm going to support Marcus and the Blues."

"I'm going to support Gaius and the Whites," said Jake.

Suddenly, two chariots charged through the triumphal arch at the end of the track. Each chariot was pulled by four horses. One charioteer, Marcus, wore blue clothes and Gaius wore white. The starter dropped a flag and the race began.

The horses rushed round the track. Marcus tried hard to get into the inside lane, but Gaius was in front. Marcus had to pull back to avoid a crash.

The crowd shouted and cheered. Half the crowd supported Gaius, and half of it supported Marcus. They waved blue and white flags. It looked like a blue-and-white sea. Sometimes, one colour was on top, and sometimes the other.

"Oh, no!" said Sophie, "Marcus is going to lose the race." But Gaius also thought that Marcus was beaten, and so he slowed down. It was a big mistake. Marcus saw his chance. He cracked the whip over the heads of his horses and dashed past Gaius. His chariot went faster and faster. Gaius tried hard but simply couldn't catch Marcus. So the Blues won!

Sophie and Jake were both shouting for their teams. They wished they had flags. Chariot races were great! Rome was great! If this was history, history was great!

"That was a great race!" said Sophie. Then suddenly the picture of the race faded, and the old city of Rome reappeared.

"What happened to Rome, Mr Johnson?" asked Jake. "Why aren't there still chariot races there?"

"Well, we can look at some dates and facts, though you might be bored by them," suggested the teacher.

"Not at all," said Jake and he clicked a button marked "CONTINUE". Whirligig came back on the screen and started to speak again.

"Chariot racing continued in Rome while the Roman Empire was strong," came Whirligig's voice.

"But, by the year AD 286, the government and army were losing power. The Empire split into East and West in AD 395 and in AD 410, people called Visigoths attacked Rome and destroyed many of its magnificent buildings. Chariots never raced in Rome again." Then Whirligig disappeared, and the computer screen went blank.

"That was great," said Jack. "Can we watch another programme next week?"

"Yes, of course," replied Mr Johnson. "I'm glad you enjoyed it."

"Thanks," said Sophie. "See you next week."

Chariots were pulled by two or four horses. This is a Roman model of a two-horse chariot, but one of the horses is missing. There could be as many as 12 chariots in a race.

Viking Explorers

The following week, Sophie and Jake were ready for more history lessons from Whirligig. Mr Johnson, their history teacher, left the two students to enjoy the CD-ROM on their own. "It's my turn to start today," said Jake.

"OK. Switch on then," said Sophie. "Which word will you type?"

"E, X, P, L, O, R, I, N, G," answered Jake as he carefully typed each letter.

On the screen, they saw wheels of numbers turning around and around. The years were rushing forwards. Slowly a picture was forming on the screen. They could see a golden sun setting over the misty sea. They could hear the sound of sea birds calling, and the wind blowing.

A wooden boat came into view. The sailors were rowing and singing with a steady rhythm. Whirligig began his explanation.

"This is Norway in the year AD 1000. A Viking longboat is returning home. The Vikings were the finest shipbuilders of their time. They sailed from their home in Scandinavia as far as Russia in the east, and North America in the west. They were great explorers. And when they discovered new places, they often attacked the natives and took their food and other possessions back to Scandinavia. They also traded with people from other countries."

The sailors sang a rhythmic song. It helped them to row steadily. Jake and Sophie wanted to row, too. It was a wonderful sound.

"Who's on the boat?" Jake wondered, "and where have they come from?" Then he pressed the video button to find out.

As the longboat sailed towards the shore, some people came out of houses nearby. The tall sail against the glowing sunset was a beautiful sight. Near the beach, a boy was standing next to a woman. She was pointing at the ship. "Look, Bjorn!" she said. "It's Seabird! Your brother Sven's ship."

"Can you see him?" Bjorn asked his mother.

"Not yet, son," she answered, "the ship isn't close enough."

Then, slowly, the longboat got nearer until the wooden bottom grated against the beach. It needed a lot of strong men from the village to pull the heavy ship onto dry land. They pulled and pulled … and suddenly it was there, on the land.

Strong warriors climbed out of the ship. They began unloading wooden chests filled with treasure. There were gold and silver cups and plates, and hundreds of gold coins.

"A fantastic expedition!" shouted one of the warriors to the people on the shore. "We got to England and found a huge monastery on a hill. One raid and now we're rich!"

The sunset scene faded, leaving behind a picture of the longboat, then Whirligig's commentary started again. There was the sound of burning fires, and screams.

"From the 8th to the 11th century, the Vikings terrorized Western Europe. They robbed and burnt villages, raided monasteries, and took cattle and treasure back home. Not all expeditions were violent raids, however. Many Vikings sailed away on peaceful trading expeditions. In fact, the Swedish Vikings, known as Varangians, traded with people around the Baltic coast, and eventually settled there."

Viking boats were tough because they were made of wood. When there was wind the Vikings put up a sail. When there was no wind, they used oars to row.

Viking warriors

These warriors are wearing chain-mail armour over leather clothes, and they're holding typical Viking weapons; shield, spear, sword, and dagger. The most frightening warriors were the berserkers, who fought furiously in battles. They believed that nothing could hurt them, so they were completely unafraid.

This dragon figurehead is from the front end of a viking ship.

A carved figurehead was often attached to the prow, or front end, of a Viking ship.

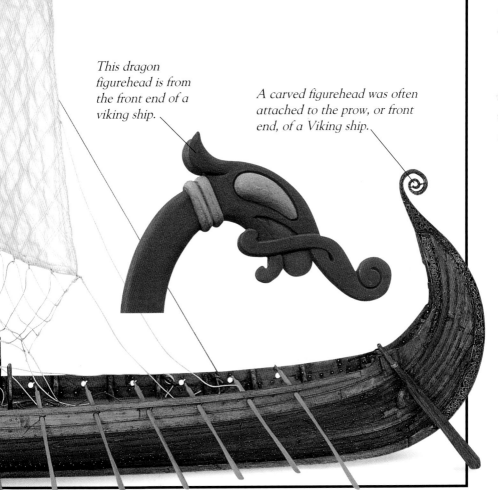

The Viking longboat disappeared off the screen, and the video button appeared. "Now press CONTINUE if you want to meet Sven, the Viking warrior," said Whirligig, the program commentator.

Sven had left the longboat and was walking along the beach towards the village. He was a tall, powerful man. He was deep in thought, and didn't even notice his young brother running to greet him.

"Sven! You're home again!" said Bjorn. "Are you happy to be back? Are you happy to see us?"

"No ... I mean, yes. Yes, Bjorn, of course I'm happy to be back. Actually, I didn't want to come home. When I was away, I met some other warriors. They had been to Greenland with Chief Eric the Red. They told me they believe there's a land further west, a land of great mountains and forests. I really want to go there."

"I wish I could go with you, Sven," said the boy.

"Well, maybe you will when you're older, Bjorn," replied Sven. "You see, no one has been there yet. Sailors have tried to land, but the wind has always been too strong."

He put an arm around his brother. "Perhaps one day we'll go together. What do you think?"

"Great! I've always wanted to sail with you on Seabird!"

Viking jewellery

"Good. I've heard that Leif the Lucky is planning an expedition to the land beyond Greenland. And I think he's planning to leave next year!"

Vikings raided, traded, or settled in these lands.

Bjorn's eyes lit up. He thought about the stories of Leif the Lucky, and the wonderful land in the west. And he felt that he, too, could travel there, far beyond the setting sun.

Bjorn was no longer a child. He felt ready to become an explorer, a real Viking, like Sven and the others.

The future was exciting and unknown. What was there beyond Greenland? An island? More land? Who lived there? People like them? Different people? And was it a cold land, or was there warm sun? "I must go," thought Bjorn, "I am a ready to be a real Viking!"

This is a modern picture of Leif standing on the prow of his ship. He is approaching the coast of North America.

The video ended. Whirligig appeared on the screen again. "Test your knowledge!" he said. "Can you remember which land Leif the Lucky discovered? Was it China, Australia, or North America?"

"Let's type in 'NORTH AMERICA,'" said Jake.

"Correct!" said Whirligig. "Leif the Lucky and his crew were the first Europeans to reach North America. They did not know that it was North America. But they knew it was a new land and they decided to stay there."

"Historians believe that Leif and his crew landed in Canada around 1002. Some Vikings even settled there for a short time. In 1960, archaeologists found the remains of an ancient settlement, with buildings in typical Viking style. This proved that the Vikings were the first Europeans to discover North America. For centuries people thought it was Christopher Columbus who had discovered this continent. He was an Italian explorer who landed on American soil in 1492. The truth is that the Vikings had been there nearly five centuries earlier. But most people still believe that Columbus discovered North America."

"Imagine sailing off and finding a new continent!" said Sophie. "The Vikings were great explorers, weren't they?"

"Yes, they were," Jake replied, "but I'm glad modern ships are different. I wouldn't like to travel to America in a Viking longboat. Imagine how dreadful it was in stormy weather. The Vikings must have been incredibly brave sailors!"

"Well, if I went to America, I would fly there," said Sophie. "I always feel sick in boats. I prefer aeroplanes – they're much faster and much more comfortable."

"Hey, you've given me an idea, Sophie. Let's type in 'flying' next."

Sophie nodded her head in agreement and typed "F, L, Y, I, N, G".

The letters jumped up and down, and Whirligig began to spin around on the screen. The rings of numbers turned around, getting faster and faster.

The Renaissance

In the middle of the computer screen a green light was shining.

"What's that light? Could it be a precious stone?" asked Sophie. She looked at the beautiful stone.

"Yes, I think it's an emerald," replied Jake. Just then a man dressed in elegant clothes appeared on the screen. He hung an emerald necklace round the neck of a young girl.

Emerald

Whirligig began to speak. "This is Lorenzo and his daughter Isabella," he said. "They're in an Italian town called Florence, and the year is 1500. It's the time known as the Renaissance, which means 'rebirth'.

At the time, European philosophers, scientists, and artists wanted to find new ways of understanding the world around them. To help them, they studied the civilization of ancient Greece and Rome. They took ideas from the great thinkers and artists of that time. Even Renaissance buildings were designed in the classical style of Greece and Rome, with their columns, arches, and domes."

"I thought we were going to learn about the history of flying," said Jake. "Should I type 'flying' again?"

"No, let's wait and see what happens next," Sophie said.

They waited. The lights flashed again, and there was music. It was very different from modern music. There was a drum and a flute … and perhaps a guitar. Sophie wasn't sure what the instruments were, but the music was magical. It was also very rhythmic, and it made Sophie want to dance.

Whirligig went on: "Human life gained new value. Before the Renaissance, religion had emphasized human weaknesses. But now there was a new movement called humanism, which emphasized human intelligence and ability.

Schools and universities were set up for medical and scientific research. And, in the world of art, a new approach to painting and drawing developed. Artists learned that objects seem smaller when they are further away from the viewer. And they drew human bodies more accurately. Rich merchants bought fine pictures and jewels as symbols of their status in society."

"I didn't know that art was connected with history," said Jake. "I like art." He clicked the video button.

Mona Lisa by Leonardo da Vinci. In Italy, the painting is known as La Gioconda. It is believed she was the wife of Francesco de Giocondo.

Many fine buildings and paintings were produced during the Renaissance.

St Peter's in Rome

The video came to life suddenly. It opened with a scene in the jeweller's shop where Lorenzo and Isabella were standing. The jeweller handed a mirror to Isabella. She looked at herself and admired the beautiful emerald that hung around her neck. "In the convent I had to wear grey," she said quietly to her father.

He smiled at her. "I know, my dear. But your school days in the convent have finished, and now you must prepare for marriage. You are fourteen, and you need fine clothes and jewels," said Lorenzo.

He gave some money to the jeweller.

"The necklace is perfect," said Lorenzo. "Very good work."

The old man looked sad. He used to make things for churches, like gold crosses with precious stones in them. Now, rich merchants like Lorenzo wanted to be more important than God, thought the jeweller.

As soon as Isabella and Lorenzo left the shop and went into the street, some thieves jumped on the merchant and tried to rob him. Lorenzo's servant pulled out a dagger and tried to protect his master. Isabella was terrified.

Lorenzo was pushed to the ground. One of the thieves pulled at his purse, which felt heavy. The thief could feel the coins inside it, and something else – perhaps jewellery. Lorenzo tried to hold on to his purse, but the thief had a sharp dagger in his hand.

Lorenzo's servant was fighting the second thief. The servant was strong, but the thief was stronger. But the servant had a dagger …

Isabella did not want to see what would happen. She turned and ran down the street as quickly as possible. Then she stopped.

She looked around and saw a small door at the end of the
street. Without even knocking, she opened it and went
through. She found herself in a small room, where a man was
working. He was looking at some drawings. Isabella stood by
the door. She was out of breath, and her heart was racing.
"Help!" Isabella shouted. "My father's in trouble! Two men
are trying to rob him!"

"Quick! Shut the door! You'll be safe in here," the man
said. "Florence is full of thieves. Let's see what's happening."
He looked out of the small window.

"It's all right. Your father is safe inside a church. I think
his servant is winning."

"Good!" said Isabella. She looked so frightened that
the man decided to talk to her about his work.

"Take a look at these drawings," he said, holding up a very big pieces of paper. They showed a man holding on to a kind of machine with wings.

"Did you draw these? Are you an artist?" asked Isabella.

"Yes, I am an artist. But no, I didn't draw the sketches. A friend of mine drew them. His name is Leonardo da Vinci," the man answered.

"But I don't understand. What are these strange wings for?" she asked. She was getting more and more interested.

"The wings are for flying. Leonardo believes people can learn to fly like birds. He's a brilliant inventor and painter. In fact, he's also a scientist, a musician, an architect and a sculptor! And I'm only a painter," he said sadly. He looked up at Isabella. She smiled at him.

"I'd like to paint a picture of you," he said, smiling again. She was wearing a dark red dress, and looked lovely.

"I'll ask my father," she said. Then remembering her father, she suddenly ran to the window and looked out. He was with his servant in the street. He was fine. The thieves had gone. "Father!" she called, "I'm here! I'm safe!"

Her father looked up. He had a cut on his head, and his hand was bleeding. But he smiled when he saw Isabella.

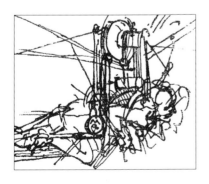

"Come up!" said Isabella, leaning out of the window. "Father, come up here! There's something wonderful here … something really strange! Come up. I want you to meet someone."

Her father smiled again, and walked towards the door.

A sketch of a flying machine, by Leonardo da Vinci.

The video stopped at this point, and the screen showed a close-up view of one of Leonardo da Vinci's sketches.

"You have to click on the sketch to get more information," said Jake.

"I'd rather find out about Isabella," said Sophie. "Do you think she'll marry a rich merchant like her father, or perhaps an artist, like that man? He was really interesting!"

But Jake wasn't interested. He had already clicked on the sketch. A light flashed, and Whirligig began to speak.

"These sketches were probably the first scientific plans for a flying machine," came Whirligig's voice. "Leonardo made them 400 years before aeroplanes were invented. The plans were found in his notebooks hundreds of years after he died.

Leonardo designed many other machines. Some of these were weapons, such as a tank that was shaped like a cockroach. Others were less dangerous, such as a parachute, a lifejacket, and a submarine. But the technology of the fifteenth century was not advanced enough for his designs. So his ideas were never developed – except for one, a design for a giant horse.

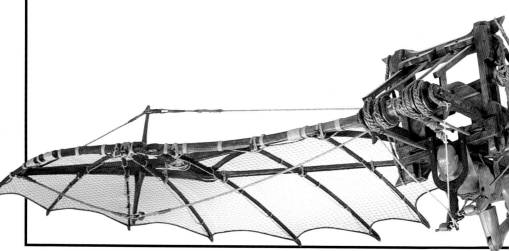

In 1482, Leonardo was invited to make a statue of a giant horse for the city of Milan, in Italy. But, in 1499, a war started, and he had to leave the city. His horse was left half-finished, and finally it was destroyed.

In 1999, 500 years later, the statue of the horse was made by Nina Akamu, a Japanese-American sculptor. It now stands in Milan, thanks to the efforts of Charles Dent, an American who raised most of the money for it."

Whirligig's voice stopped speaking, and the screen went dark. Rings of numbers started to appear, going around and around in circles. There was more music, and more lights. Where would they go next?

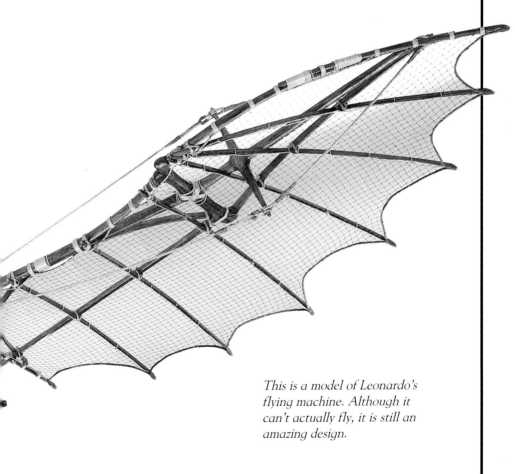

This is a model of Leonardo's flying machine. Although it can't actually fly, it is still an amazing design.

Gold Rush

"Did you like Isabella's dress?" asked Jake.

"It was a beautiful colour, but I wouldn't like to wear it," said Sophie. "I prefer a T-shirt and jeans."

"I wonder why they're called 'jeans'," said Jake. "Do you think they were invented by someone called Jean?"

"Perhaps somebody called Jean was the first person to wear them," suggested Sophie. "Let's see if Whirligig has the answer. He knows everything!"

She typed in "Jeans". Whirligig's spinning rings became wagon wheels, travelling across mountains and deserts. Then his voice began to explain:

"In 1848, gold was discovered in California, on the west coast of America. In 1849, thousands of people rushed from the other side of America in search of a fortune – they were called 'forty-niners'. By 1850, there were many mining towns full of disappointed people who had found nothing. A few lucky ones became very rich. Life was hard and dangerous – those who found gold often lost it in the gambling houses. Or their gold was stolen by other people. Everyone wanted gold, and they would do anything to get it. It was a violent society and a cruel one."

"In this video, you'll see two orphans, Ellen and Clem, arriving at a mining town."

"But what about jeans?" asked Jake. "I don't see why we're hearing about gold mining."

"Be patient," said Sophie, and she clicked the video button. The wagon wheels turned and turned and became a wagon pulled by two thin horses.

A girl and a boy were sitting in the wagon, shivering in the cold. They had just reached a town of tents and huts. The streets were muddy, and the puddles were frozen.

A dirty unshaven man came up to the wagon.

"You'd better go back east. That's where you belong," he said. "They call this town Miseryville."

"It's horrible," moaned Ellen. "Let's go back. We'll never get rich here."

"We can't go home now," said Clem. "We've come too far, and we've spent all our money. Tomorrow, I'll look for gold. If I can just find one nugget, we'll be rich for the rest of our lives! Come on, Ellen. You'll feel better in the morning, when you've had some sleep."

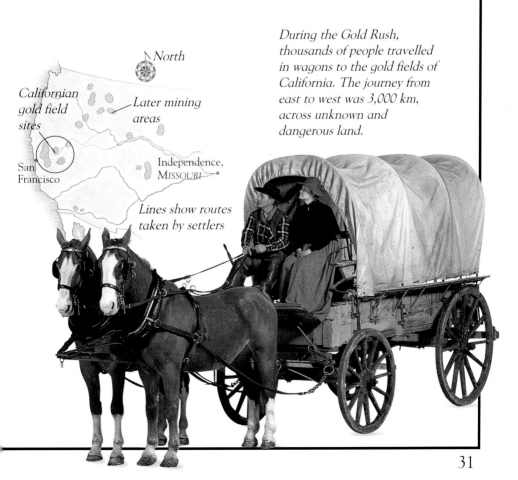

North

Californian gold field sites

Later mining areas

San Francisco

Independence, MISSOURI

Lines show routes taken by settlers

During the Gold Rush, thousands of people travelled in wagons to the gold fields of California. The journey from east to west was 3,000 km, across unknown and dangerous land.

Clem spent the next day at the river. At first, he couldn't reach the bank because there were so many other forty-niners. Finally, he found a space and dipped his pan into the freezing water. He swirled it around and waited for it to settle. He was sure that he would see gold shining in the mud. But there was no gold. Just water and mud. Clem felt cold.

A prospector looks at his pan. He would quickly see any gold because it was heavy and sank to the bottom of the pan.

It was the same story all that day, and for many days after: no gold. Ellen started to despair. Soon the snow would come, and she was already so cold in her thin dress.

She was saved by a friendly neighbour, the wife of a prospector.

"You look frozen," she said. "Why don't you wear these?" She handed over a pair of blue trousers. "Mr Levi Strauss makes them for the prospectors."

"Trousers!" said Ellen. "I can't wear those! Only men wear trousers."

"If you don't, you'll freeze to death for sure," said the prospector's wife. She smiled at Ellen. "A dress might be OK for the city, but out here you need tough, warm trousers."

Ellen hesitated. Trousers? For a woman? She could not wear them. But then she shivered again. The wind was getting colder and colder. It went straight through her thin dress like a knife.

She held out her hands. "Thank you," she said. "You're right. I'll go and put them on!"

Ellen went back into the wagon and put on the trousers. They were rough, but so warm! Suddenly, she felt better.

"Clem will want something hot to eat when he gets back," she said to herself. She made batter from corn flour and eggs, and she began to cook some pancakes. The pancakes turned golden in the pan, and the smell rose into the air.

Tough trousers
Jeans are made of denim, a blue cotton cloth, which is very strong and hard-wearing. Levi Strauss, from Bavaria in Germany, began making jeans for prospectors in 1850. He became an extremely rich man.

A prospector walked past on his way back from a successful day at the river. He sniffed the air.

"Those pancakes smell good, Miss. I'll give you a pinch of gold dust if you'll make one for me." Soon a whole group of forty-niners had arrived at Ellen and Clem's wagon. They stood around it in a circle.

"Have you got enough for everybody, Miss?" asked a hopeful prospector.

Ellen made pancake after pancake. By the time Clem got back, there was just enough batter left to make one pancake for him. But she had more gold dust than Clem had found in all his days on the river.

"You can forget the river, Clem," she called to him, "there's an easier way to find gold." She tossed Clem's pancake high in the air. As it flipped over, Whirligig's circles filled the screen, and the voice began to speak:

"Levi Strauss was a German who went to California with a wagon full of strong cotton cloth. He planned to make tents. Then he saw that the prospectors needed strong warm clothes, so he made trousers instead. It just happened that the cloth was blue. Why were they called jeans? Because the cloth came from Genoa. So American jeans were invented by a German and named after an Italian city! They are really international! They are still worn in almost every country in the world. They are worn by people of all ages … and all shapes! People love their jeans, and go on wearing them even when they are no longer new."

"California grew to be large and rich. By 1849, the population had risen from 20,000 to 100,000, and it kept on growing. Many of the prospectors settled in the state, and farmers, traders and salesmen joined them. Towns, roads and railways were built."

"Now I'm hungry," said Jake, thinking about Ellen's pancakes. He pressed the "STOP" button. Just then, Mr Johnson came into the room. "Is it good? Are you learning anything?" the teacher asked.

"It's really interesting," said Sophie. "It's not like normal history lessons. We're discovering a lot of new things."

"It's not as exciting as real films, though," said Jake. "I watched a good film last night. It was about soldiers in the war. It wasn't like history, because it was about real people."

"Well, let's see if Whirligig can tell us about that," said Mr Johnson, and typed in "SECOND WORLD WAR". Then he pressed "PAUSE". There were the usual lights, moving numbers, and music. Sophie and Jake waited.

A busy mining town during the Gold Rush.

World War II

"Your grandparents were probably teenagers in the war," said Mr Johnson. "They must have lots of interesting memories."

"My grandfather told me it was really miserable. People were always hungry, and children never had any sweets," said Jake. "And there was no fruit or cakes."

"But the American soldiers were popular. They often gave people chocolate. My grandmother used to say, 'Got any gum, chum?' Then they gave her a stick of chewing gum!'", said Sophie. Mr Johnson clapped his hands with delight.

"That's what history's all about – the lives of real people! Now let's get some facts about World War II." He pressed the "START" button.

Whirligig's rings filled the screen as it turned blue. Then two aeroplanes dived out of the sky and bombs exploded. Whirligig's information began:

"Adolf Hitler became leader of Germany in 1934. He wanted to expand German territory. In 1939, Germany invaded Poland, and Britain and France declared war. By 1940, Germany had conquered most of mainland Europe. German submarines sank many ships that were bringing food to Britain. German planes bombed British cities. And British planes bombed German cities.

"America came into the war in 1941, and eventually 1.5 million American troops were living in camps in Britain. What did the British think of them? Watch the video. It shows an American soldier meeting a British family."

Sophie clicked the video button eagerly.

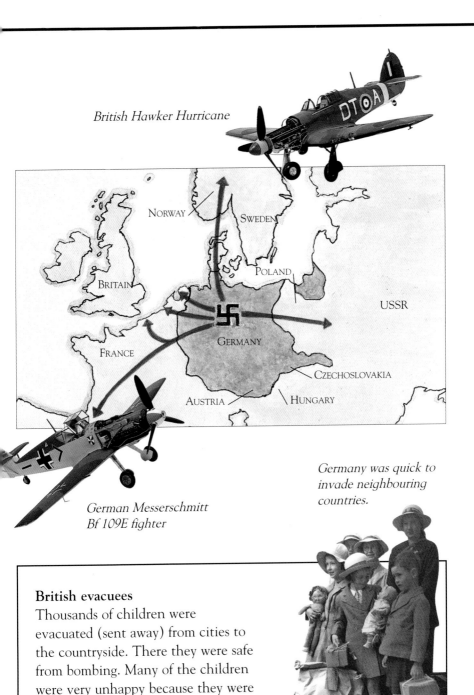

British Hawker Hurricane

NORWAY

SWEDEN

POLAND

BRITAIN

USSR

GERMANY

FRANCE

CZECHOSLOVAKIA

AUSTRIA

HUNGARY

German Messerschmitt Bf 109E fighter

Germany was quick to invade neighbouring countries.

British evacuees

Thousands of children were evacuated (sent away) from cities to the countryside. There they were safe from bombing. Many of the children were very unhappy because they were so far from home. So, after a short time, they returned home.

The scene showed a boy and his mother standing next to a table. The boy looked miserable. His clothes were old and worn out. His mother looked tired. The night before, they hadn't slept because of the bombs. The boy's mother had put sticky tape on the windows to stop the glass breaking when the bombs exploded. It was the boy's birthday but he was not enjoying it. The boy and his mother were staring at each other. It was not a happy scene.

On the table there was a plate of sandwiches and a small plain cake.

The boy was complaining: "This isn't a proper birthday party, Mum! We ought to have jelly and ice cream. There aren't even any candles on the cake. It doesn't feel like my birthday at all."

"Food is rationed, you know," said his mother. "Clothes, too. We don't get much for the coupons in our ration books. I've done my best. I've used all the family's sugar ration in that cake. And there are no candles for sale in the shops."

Just then his older sister came in.

"Susan!" David shouted. "Have you got me a present?" Susan gave him a pencil and a card saying "Happy Birthday", which she'd made herself. David was upset.

"It's not fair! I haven't even had any chocolate. You used to get proper presents when you were my age. If only I could have a bike like Susan's!"

"There's a war on!" cried his mother. "Blame Hitler, not your poor sister."

Susan burst into tears. "I wish Dad was here. You're selfish! We've tried to give you a birthday, and you can't say 'Thank you'. You're really selfish, David! Dad would be really disappointed!"

She ran out of the front door and immediately bumped into a soldier.

"Hey! What's wrong?" the soldier asked. Susan looked up at him. He wasn't dressed like a British soldier. His uniform was a lighter colour.

"Everything's wrong!" she said. "It's my brother's birthday, and there are no toys and sweets, so he's cross. We haven't got enough food for a proper party. Dad's away in the army!"

"Maybe good old Uncle Sam can help," said the soldier.

"You're American!" said Susan. She was very surprised. She hadn't met an American before.

"Sure. I'm Clark. I'm from the US base down the road. I guess we can spare a bit of food for a boy's birthday party. After all, you British say we're 'overpaid, overfed, and over here!'"

Half an hour later Clark was back with lots of good things – tins of ham and fruit, butter, chewing gum, oranges. This was unbelievable in wartime Britain.

The two children and their mother looked at each other. Their eyes were shining. They had not seen food like this for a long time. It was like a dream.

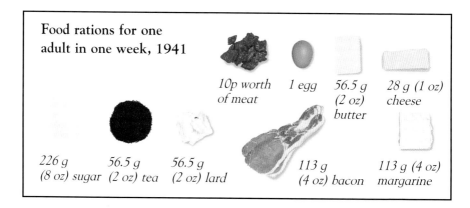

Food rations for one adult in one week, 1941

10p worth of meat

1 egg

56.5 g (2 oz) butter

28 g (1 oz) cheese

226 g (8 oz) sugar

56.5 g (2 oz) tea

56.5 g (2 oz) lard

113 g (4 oz) bacon

113 g (4 oz) margarine

"This is a real treat you know," said David's mother, as she opened the tin of ham. "Please stay and join the party, Clark."

"I'd like that," he said. "And here's a special present for you, David."

The American soldier gave him a big box of chocolates. As David passed the box round, Whirligig began to spin again.

"In 1944, British and American troops landed in France," the voice explained, "and the Germans began to retreat. France, Holland, and Belgium were liberated. Russian troops invaded Germany from the east, and eventually captured Berlin. Hitler committed suicide and, in May 1945, Germany surrendered.

"Perhaps Susan married Clark and became a 'GI bride'. 70,000 British women married American soldiers and went back to the USA with them. Even when the war ended, life was still hard for people throughout Europe. Millions had died. Many houses and factories were destroyed in the bombing and the fighting. There was a shortage of almost everything. In Britain, food rationing continued until 1953."

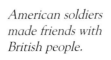

American soldiers made friends with British people.

Space Age

"World War II was terrible," said Sophie. "Do you think countries will ever learn to live together peacefully?"

"They might – one day," said Jake. "Let's find out what happens when people leave the Earth and explore other planets." He typed "SPACE EXPLORATION".

Whirligig's voice began:

"The first man-made satellite was launched in October 1957 by the Soviet Union. It was called Sputnik I. The next month, they sent the first living creature into orbit – a dog called Laika. From then on, it was a race between the USSR and America to put the first man into space. The USSR won the race when some amazing news was reported on 12 April 1961: Yuri Gagarin had completed a single orbit of the Earth.

The Americans won a different race on 20 July 1969 when their space craft landed on the Moon. As Neil Armstrong walked on to the Moon's dusty surface, he took "one small step for man and one giant leap for mankind."

Space probes
Probes are unmanned spacecrafts. They carry cameras and other equipment for exploring space. Data is sent back to Earth. The Galileo probe took off in 1989 to explore the planet Jupiter.

Galileo probe

"Even in space, countries compete instead of helping one another," sighed Sophie.

Whirligig went on: "The Russians launched the first space station, Salyut in 1971. Then the Americans followed it with Skylab. The most successful space station was the Russian Mir, which meant 'peace'. Astronauts of many nations, including Britain and America, spent time on Mir before it crashed back into the Earth's atmosphere.

The next space station will be truly international. In fact, it will be called the International Space Station, and many nations, including both Russia and America, will build parts of it. It should be completed in 2004."

"That's too many facts," said Jake. "Let's watch the video".

He clicked on "VIDEO". Instead of the planets and rockets they expected to see, they saw a man in old-fashioned clothes, looking through a primitive telescope.

"This is Jean Cassini," said Whirligig, "who first discovered three moons around the planet Saturn. He lived in the seventeenth century."

The picture faded, and a boy and a girl in modern clothes appeared on the screen. They were in a classroom.

"The United States, 1996," explained Whirligig. "Meet Joe and Kate. Kate's very proud because she's going to fly to Saturn!" The girl was laughing.

"Of course, you're not going to fly to Saturn," said Joe. "That's an absolute lie!"

"It's nearly true," laughed Kate. "I found a website about the Cassini project. It asked people to send in their signatures, so I did. People even sent in their dog's paw prints. They put them all on a disc. It will be carried in the spacecraft when it goes to Saturn. So part of me will fly to Saturn!"

"So if there are people on Saturn – and they have computers that can read the disc – they'll discover what your name is," said Joe, laughing at Kate.

"That's a big deal!"

"If you studied harder in science lessons, you would know there aren't any people on Saturn," Kate replied. "It's almost all gases like hydrogen and helium. And another thing, Cassini's not going to land on Saturn – it will send a probe to explore one of Saturn's moons, called Titan. When it has sent back enough information about Titan and Saturn, it will go off into deep space. In some distant galaxy, an alien being will read my name and wonder what sort of creature I am."

"No wonder Kate was excited," said Sophie. Jake pressed the "Pause" button. He looked puzzled.

"I've never heard of the Cassini project. I'd like to know more," he said, and typed in "CASSINI".

The screen showed a huge rocket, soaring off its launch pad. Soon it was just a tiny spot of light in the sky.

"October, 1977," came Whirligig's voice, "Cape Canaveral, USA. Watch this!"

"A Titan 4 rocket is being launched, carrying the Cassini spacecraft. It is setting off on a long, long journey to Saturn, which will take seven years. America and many European countries worked together on the project. It is hoped that Cassini will dramatically advance our knowledge of the galaxy. The cost of sending a spacecraft to Saturn is an amazing $3.3 billion!"

Jake and Sophie looked at each other. $3.3 billion! How much was that in "real" money – money that they could understand? They had no idea, but it was obviously an enormous amount of money. They had heard their parents talking about the money the Government should spend on things. They talked about millions or billions of dollars, too.

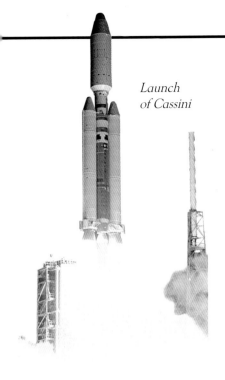

Launch of Cassini

"The Cassini project is controversial, and not just because of the cost. Because Saturn is so far from the sun, Cassini's batteries can't be charged by solar power. So it carries 30 kilos of plutonium. What would happen if the spacecraft crashed back into the earth's atmosphere?

"Even after the successful launch, there were protests in many countries. But the protests were not in the US! The video will show you why."

The screen changed to show a very different classroom.

"This is a science lesson in Bangladesh, in August 1999," said Whirligig. "Look carefully."

"The teacher is telling the class about the Cassini spacecraft. It's important in Bangladesh, too."

"Even the Titan rocket was not powerful enough to send Cassini to Saturn," said the teacher. "It has to use the gravity of two planets to give it enough speed. After almost two years, it is heading back to Earth at 70,000 kilometres an hour. If it enters Earth's atmosphere, it will burn up. This means that radiation could spread across many countries, including Bangladesh. It is a terrible risk."

Cassini spacecraft

This is an artist's picture of the space probe as it leaves the Cassini spacecraft in 2004. It is shown flying over Titan, Saturn's largest moon.

One boy put up his hand to speak.

"But Sir," he said, "it is also a great adventure. The people of Earth must explore space. Mankind's best hope for the future lies in space travel."

"I don't think it's worth the risk," said the girl next to him. "It's a waste of money, as well. Think of all the good things you could do on Earth if you had $3.3 billion."

Whirligig's rings filled the screen once more.

"Fortunately, Cassini did not crash into the Earth, and is safely on its way to Saturn. But the arguments will continue.

In 2003, the Europa Orbiter will be launched to study one of Jupiter's moons, and that will also carry radioactive power. Some people say that an accident could destroy life on Earth. Others say that exploration of space is essential, because one day Earth's resources will be used up.

Some people think the money should be spent on ending poverty and disease on Earth. Others say that the advance of space technology benefits all mankind. What do you think?"

The screen went dark, and the words "End of Programme" appeared. Sophie and Jake sighed.

"Well," said Mr Johnson, "what do you think? That sounds like a good question for your next homework."

"But Sir," said Jake and Sophie together, "that's not history. That's the future. That would be a good question for history homework in the year 3000!"

Mr Johnson smiled at them. "So, you see," he said, "history is about the past, the present, and the future. It never stops. That's why it's so exciting."

Glossary and Key People

Ancient Rome
The period when Rome was a very important city and governed many other states.

BC and AD
BC means "Before Christ" – the years before Christ was born. AD means "Anno Domini" (in the year of our Lord) – the years after Christ was born.

chariot races
Races for carts pulled by horses.

charioteer
The person who drove the chariot. Charioteers were often slaves.

Circus Maximus
A huge racetrack for chariot races in Ancient Rome. 250,000 people could watch the races there.

Emperor
The ruler of an empire, like Napoleon.

Empire
A group of countries ruled by one country, e.g. the Roman Empire or the British Empire.

Eric the Red
A Viking leader who explored Greenland in AD 984 and 985.

Hitler, Adolf
The leader of Germany between 1933 and 1945, before and during the Second World War.

Legions
The Roman army was divided into legions. Each legion had about 5,000 soldiers.

Leif the Lucky
The son of Eric the Red. He was the first European to land in North America, in about AD 1001.

Leonardo da Vinci
A great artist and inventor who lived in Italy from 1452–1519.

longboat
A Viking warship.

merchants
Business people who made money by buying and selling things.

prospectors
People who went to look for gold.

raiders
People who made quick attacks on towns and villages, stealing cows, treasure, and slaves.

Ration
A small amount of food that each person can have during a war.

slaves
People who "belong to" other people. They could be bought and sold.

Strauss, Levi
In 1873, he was the first person to make and sell jeans.

traders
People who exchanged things like gold, silver, and furs for other things.

tribe
A "large family", like the Sioux in North America.

Vikings
People from Scandinavia who explored the North Atlantic and went to England, Northern France, and Sicily.

Visigoths
A German tribe.

warriors
Soldiers in a tribe.